Access your online resources

The **Glitter Jar**, **Coping Chatterbox**, **Home Is Where the Heart Is**, and **Awards Ceremony** pages are available online to be downloaded and
printed for easy use.

Go to https://resourcecentre.routledge.com/speechmark and click on the cover of this book.

Answer the question prompt using your copy of the book to gain access to the online content.

"My Residential School Trip Activity Book and *Guide* are fantastic resources for young explorers to find their courage. These books assist children in building their bravery backpacks for a lifetime of adventures."

Robert Swan *OBE, FRGS – Polar explorer, the first person in history to walk to both the North and South Pole.*

My Residential School Trip Activity Book

My Residential School Trip Activity Book *is most effective when delivered alongside the accompanying* My Residential School Trip Facilitator's Guide.

This activity book is designed for 7–12-year-olds and is full of engaging, strength-based activities that encourage the child to colour, decorate, and annotate the book to make it their own, as well as to reflect on how they feel about their forthcoming trip.

The text normalises worry as a response to something new and helps children to understand their worries and build bravery as they work through the book. Pages look at how to get ready for the trip and compile a 'toolbox' of effective coping skills to embrace challenge. The book also provides an opportunity for post-trip reflection and concludes with activities that bring together the journey through the pages, helping to solidify engagement with the text and increase wellbeing and self-esteem.

Best introduced about eight weeks before departure, this is a must-have resource to help children build bravery, so that they have the best experience on their residential school trip.

Claire Holmes is a school counsellor. Her approach is trauma-informed and strength-based, empowering others to access their inner wisdom and knowing. As a mindfulness teacher, she weaves meditation into her work, alongside expressive therapies and solution-focused interventions. She delights in spending time in the great outdoors and is a nature and forest therapy guide. She's passionate about the positive impact of school trips. Having lived and worked in Singapore for over two decades, she has accompanied countless overseas and local expeditions. She is the author of the *Moving On* and *Staying Well* series, and is delighted to add the *My Residential School Trip* books to her collection.

This book is part of a set –

Book 1: *My Residential School Trip Activity Book* is jam packed full of practical activities that invite the reader to use their creativity by annotating and illustrating the pages. Alongside practical considerations, the children will explore feelings, notice where these are felt in their bodies, and compile a 'toolbox' of effective coping skills to embrace challenge.

Book 2: *My Residential School Trip Facilitator's Guide* offers guidance notes and prompts to help the facilitator bring out the best experience for the child using *My Residential School Trip Activity Book*. It includes key points to consider, examples of what to say, and explains the theory behind the activities as well as offering practical extension ideas.

My Residential School Trip

Practical Activities to Help Children Aged 7–12 Build Bravery for the Best Time

Claire Holmes

Routledge
Taylor & Francis Group

LONDON AND NEW YORK

Designed cover image: Lisa Dynan

First published 2025

by Routledge
4 Park Square, Milton Park, Abingdon, Oxon OX14 4RN

and by Routledge
605 Third Avenue, New York, NY 10158

Routledge is an imprint of the Taylor & Francis Group, an informa business

© 2025 Claire Holmes

The right of Claire Holmes to be identified as author of this work has been asserted in accordance with sections 77 and 78 of the Copyright, Designs and Patents Act 1988.

British Library Cataloguing-in-Publication Data
A catalogue record for this book is available from the British Library

ISBN: 978-1-032-84025-3 (pbk)
ISBN: 978-1-003-51085-7 (ebk)
This book can also be purchased as part of a set: *My Residential School Trip*, 9781032840222 (set)

DOI: 10.4324/9781003510857

Typeset in Tekton Pro
by Deanta Global Publishing Services, Chennai, India

Access the Support Material: https://resourcecentre.routledge.com/speechmark

Acknowledgements

To my school trip buddies over the years both students and staff, I am so thankful for the experiences and places we have seen. Shout out to my school counselling colleagues, past and present. Your wisdom is in these pages. Gratitude to my Expressive Therapy guru, the ever-wise, Helen Wilson. Last, but not least, kudos to family Holmes for our South-East Asian adventures. Brave times indeed.

Notes to parents

Each time I am lucky enough to attend a school trip I am humbled and awestruck by the positive impact on the children. The independence, confidence, and social interaction gains are often astounding. However, it's natural for some children to feel nervous about being away from home, especially if they haven't done it before. Your support is invaluable in getting them ready for the off, here are some tips to help with this:

Get yourself comfortable: Ensure you are calm before talking to your child, especially if you are worried about the trip yourself. Your attitude will directly correlate with your child's; your confidence can help boost theirs. Practice self-care, speak to supportive people in your life about your worries. Avoid voicing concerns about your child being away in front of them. If possible, connect with other parents who are grounded and positive about the trip.

Communicate openly: Listen to your child's concerns about the trip without judgement. Ask questions to understand their worries better and offer reassurance. Listen more than you talk and keep the door open for ongoing conversations. Liaise with the school in good time, let them know that your child is worried about the trip and see what support they can offer.

Provide information: Sometimes, children are worried because they don't know what to expect. Share as much information as you can about the trip such as the itinerary, the supportive people going, the activities planned, and the kit list. Sleeping arrangements and groupings are often a concern for children.

Talk about coping strategies: Discuss strategies your child can use to build bravery. For example, deep breathing, grounding, chatting to a friend, talking with a supportive adult, or focusing on the positive aspects of the trip. Let them know you are confident they can cope and working through this activity book will show them how.

Reassure of safety: Remind your child the trip has been planned carefully and there will be adults around to keep them safe.

Focus on the positives: Help your child see the fun and exciting parts of the trip, such as exploring new places, learning new things, and spending time with friends.

Pack familiar items: Allow your child to bring a comfort item, such as a favourite stuffed animal or blanket, to help them feel more at ease during the trip. You may like to consider giving them an item of yours to create a sense of connectedness while they are away. Some parents write short letters for the child to open during the trip, offer a family photo or some sort of reminder of home.

Keep in touch: Explain the plan for communication while they are away and that you can be contacted in an emergency.

Practice separation: If your child struggles with separation, practice small separations leading up to the trip to help them get used to being away from home. Sleepovers with peers are a great way to do this.

Set realistic expectations: Let your child know it's okay to feel a little nervous or homesick, and these feelings will likely pass as they enjoy the trip.

Logistics: Talk with your child about the day of departure and what will happen. On the day, keep yourself steady, try not to rush, create a positive pre-departure atmosphere, and be safe in the knowledge that this is an opportunity for your child (and you) to grow. Don't forget to plan their return and how you'll celebrate their successful trip.

Welcome!

You've been given this activity book because you are going on a residential trip. Doing something new and staying away from home is both exciting and challenging. The activities in this book will help you prepare for the trip by building bravery. You'll get creative by drawing, colouring, writing, and making things. Pages 1–30 are to be filled in before your trip and pages 31–34 will help you celebrate your successful return.

This book belongs to_____

My school trip is to_____

I will travel there and back by _____

I'll be staying there for_____nights.

Residential means you'll be sleeping overnight for one night or more.

Adventure awaits!
You are the best version of yourself when you awaken bravery and courage.

Being brave

It's normal to have worries about your trip. When you worry about an event it's a sure sign you are going to do something brave. The more often you notice your bravery, the easier it will be to find. Let's think about a time you were brave.

Fill in the gaps.

I was brave when I: _____

Draw something above to go with this time of being brave.
Write something below that helped you cope:

Hopes and fears flower

It's normal to have hopes and fears about the trip.

Write or draw a fear about the trip in each petal and your hopes in the centre of the flower.

Some will be the same as your friends going with you and some will be unique to you.

Unique means special to you.

Awakening strengths

Bravery is a strength that everyone has inside of them. We all have many strengths; these are positive character traits that you and others notice. Using your strengths helps you be the best version of yourself.

Here are some examples of strengths:

Kind, caring, funny, patient, trusting, friendly, grateful, loyal, helpful, joyful, honest, determined, brave, creative, respectful, and peaceful.

Character traits are qualities that make you who you are.

Write other strengths you can think of here:

Strengths you take everywhere

Your strengths are your superpowers!

1) Write your strengths inside the body outline above. Aim for eight or more.

2) In the box below, write three strengths you wrote in your body outline that are most important to help you go on the trip.

3) In the box below, write one strength that you did not add to your body outline that would help you go on the trip.

TRY THIS: When you feel challenged, pause, take a breath, and think about which strengths you can awaken.

Get curious

Getting curious about the trip will build bravery.

Ask your teachers, trip leader, someone who has been on the trip already, and/or parent(s)/guardian some questions. Here are some examples (use your hopes and fears flower to help you think of more).

- What activities will we be doing?
- Where will we sleep?
- Who will drop me off and collect me?
- What food will we eat?
- How many people will be in my group?
- What do I need to bring, do we have a kit list?

Start packing early to make sure you have everything you need.

If you have other questions you'd like to ask, write them in the box below:

I am looking forward to...

1) Write down five things you are looking forward to about the trip on the lines below:

_____

_____

_____

_____

_____

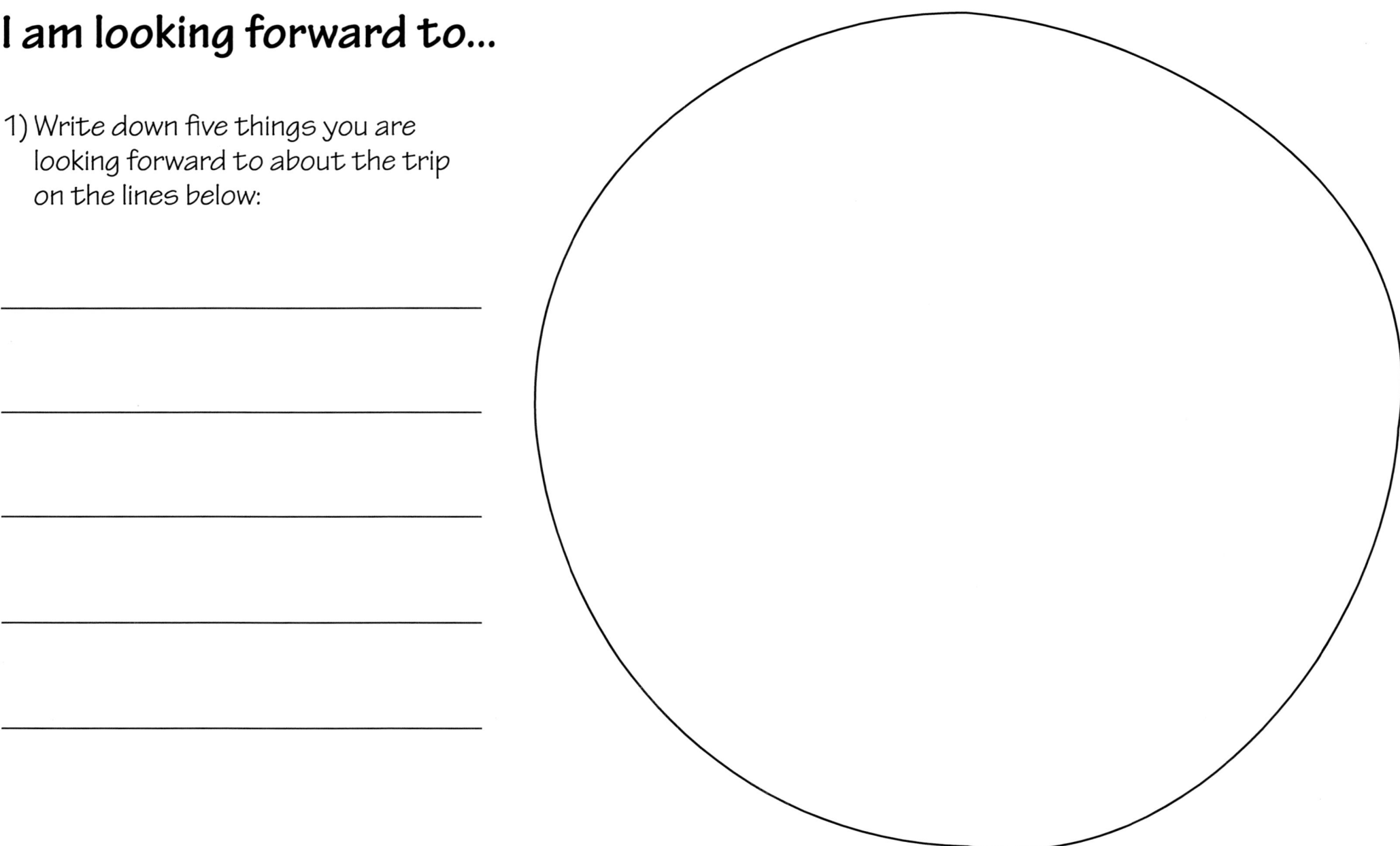

2) Draw a pattern in circle above (colours, shapes, lines, dots, and/or squiggles) to represent what you are looking forward to during the trip.

What to do when big feelings arrive

Taking care of big feelings makes room for bravery. If you take care of feeling worried or scared, it is possible to feel brave at the same time. Here's a formula for taking care of feelings: N^3. There are three **N**s to remember. Each has a question that goes with it.

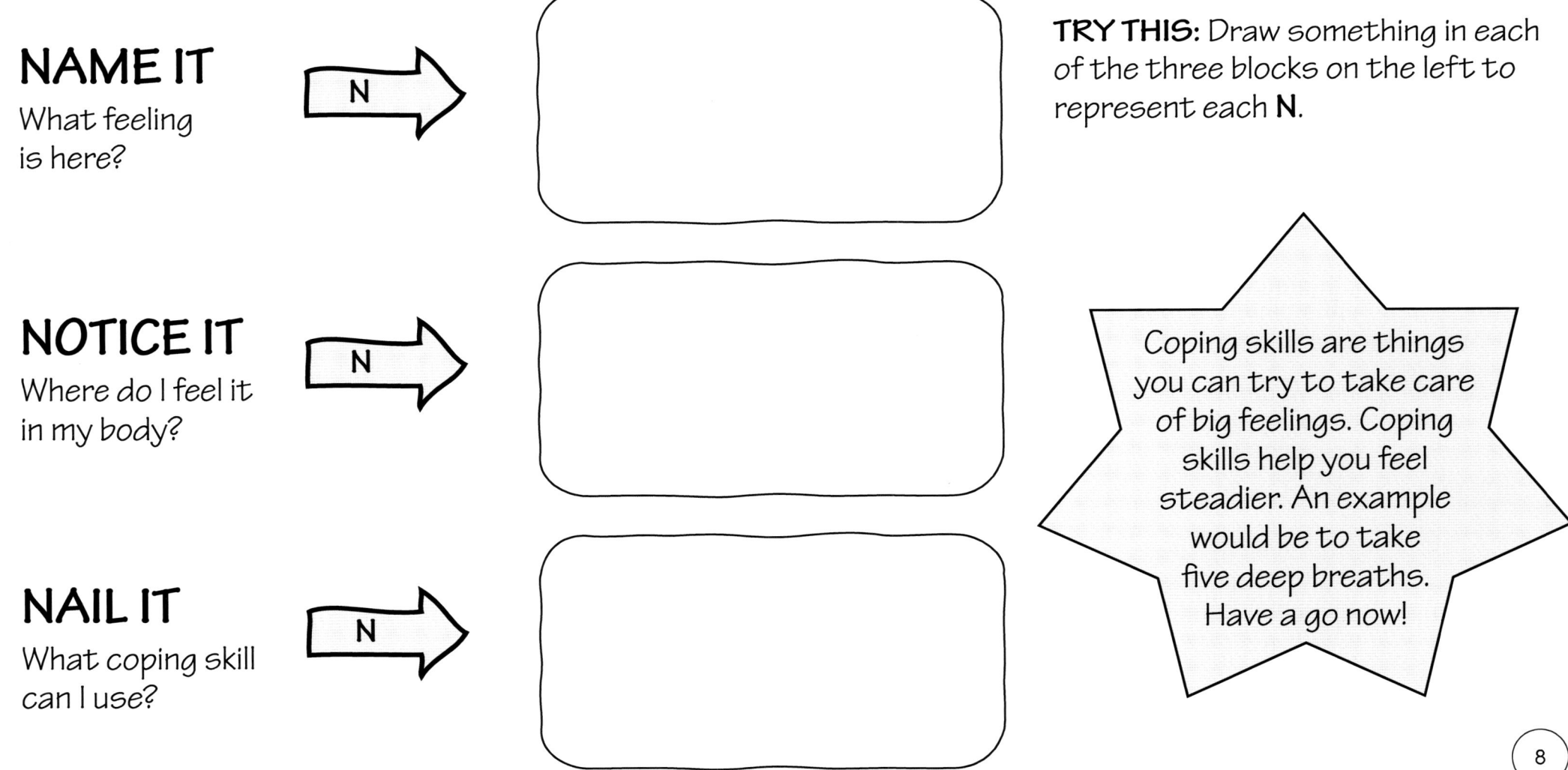

NAME IT
What feeling is here?

N

TRY THIS: Draw something in each of the three blocks on the left to represent each **N**.

NOTICE IT
Where do I feel it in my body?

N

NAIL IT
What coping skill can I use?

N

Coping skills are things you can try to take care of big feelings. Coping skills help you feel steadier. An example would be to take five deep breaths. Have a go now!

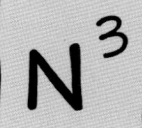

1) Can you remember the first **N** from the **N³** formula?

Fill in the gaps below (use page 8 to help you if you need to):

The first **N** is for _____

The question that goes with it is (it's on page 8):

_____

Finding feelings

2) The feelings below are somewhere in the wordsearch. Words are hidden ⇨ ⇩ and ⬊. How many can you find?

ANGRY   LONELY

BRAVE   MAD

CONFUSED   SAD

ENERGISED   SCARED

EXCITED   STRONG

FURIOUS   UPSET

GLAD   WORRIED

I	P	K	J	A	G	H	O	P	E	F	U	L	Y	V	M	S	F
X	P	E	A	C	E	F	U	L	A	C	L	X	M	M	G	C	C
U	A	V	I	M	K	E	X	H	N	O	E	B	S	A	A	A	K
Y	U	S	I	W	W	N	M	F	P	N	X	L	A	P	N	R	S
P	P	K	J	A	O	E	C	C	I	F	C	F	D	C	G	E	T
B	S	E	U	L	B	R	A	V	E	U	I	J	X	U	R	D	R
E	E	A	Y	O	B	G	R	K	W	S	T	G	X	R	Y	U	O
H	T	L	U	N	M	I	B	I	A	E	E	W	G	I	C	M	N
T	V	E	J	E	M	S	C	K	E	D	D	E	L	O	A	Z	G
M	E	C	Q	L	A	E	C	B	I	D	F	I	A	U	L	M	H
O	X	U	H	Y	D	D	Y	Z	H	G	P	O	D	S	M	O	R
B	U	F	U	R	I	O	U	S	U	B	I	Z	L	O	K	X	Z

TRY THIS: Look around you and find as many things as you can that start with the same letter as the first feeling you found.

Feelings wheel

Choose six big feelings you have about your trip (use the last page to help if you need to).

Write one of them in each section of the circle on the right. Colour each section of your feelings wheel.

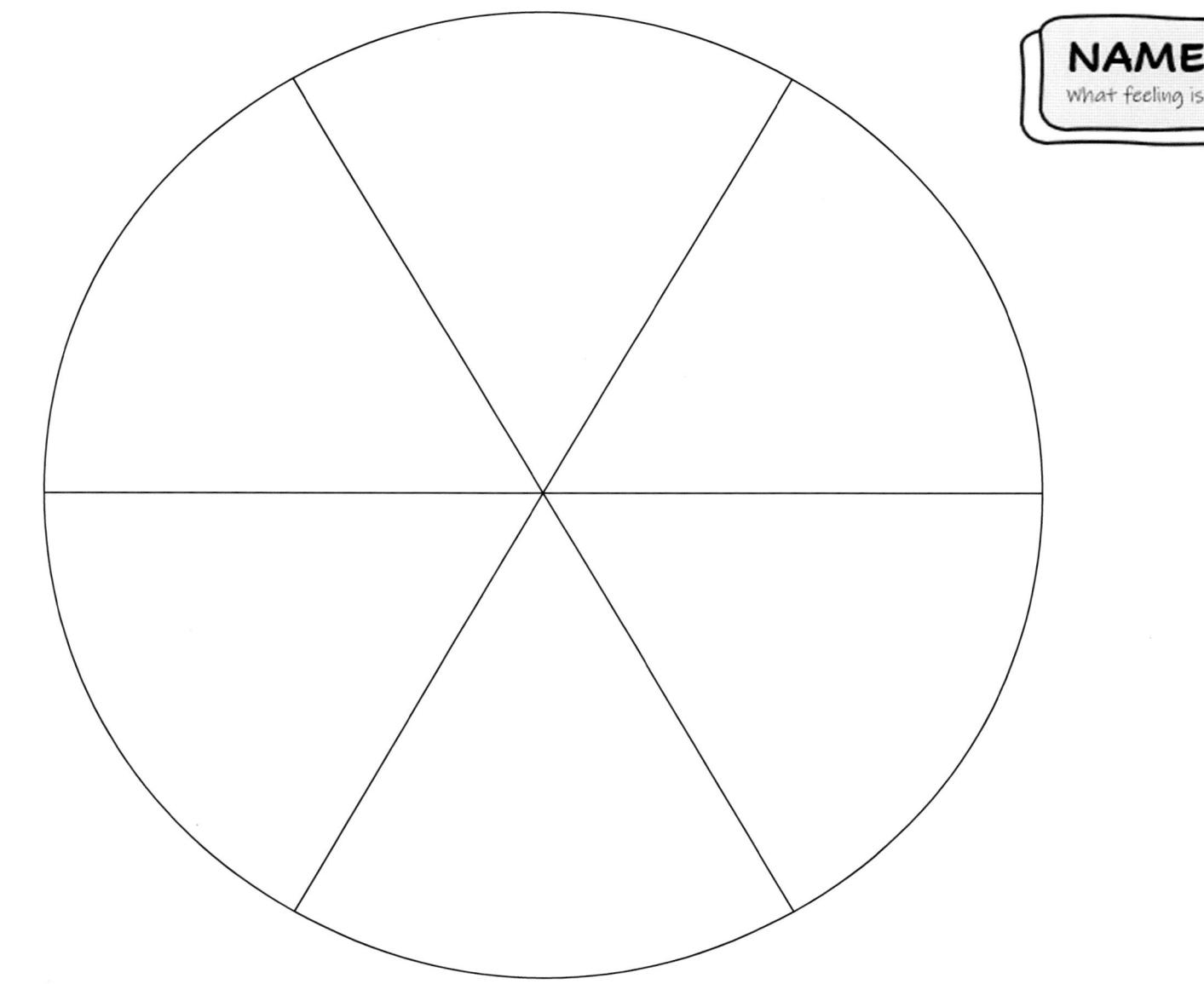

Remember: Feelings are like postmen; they deliver important information.

Feelings come and go, they are not good or bad.

N³ Fill in the gaps (look at page 8 if you need to):

The second **N** is for

_____

The question that goes
with it is (it's on page 8):

_____

_____

Listen to your body

Your body will let you know when big feelings arrive. Every body is different. Take your six big feelings from the last page and draw symbols, colours, shapes, lines, or squiggles where you feel them in your own body inside the outline on the right. Add some labels to explain and any other details too.

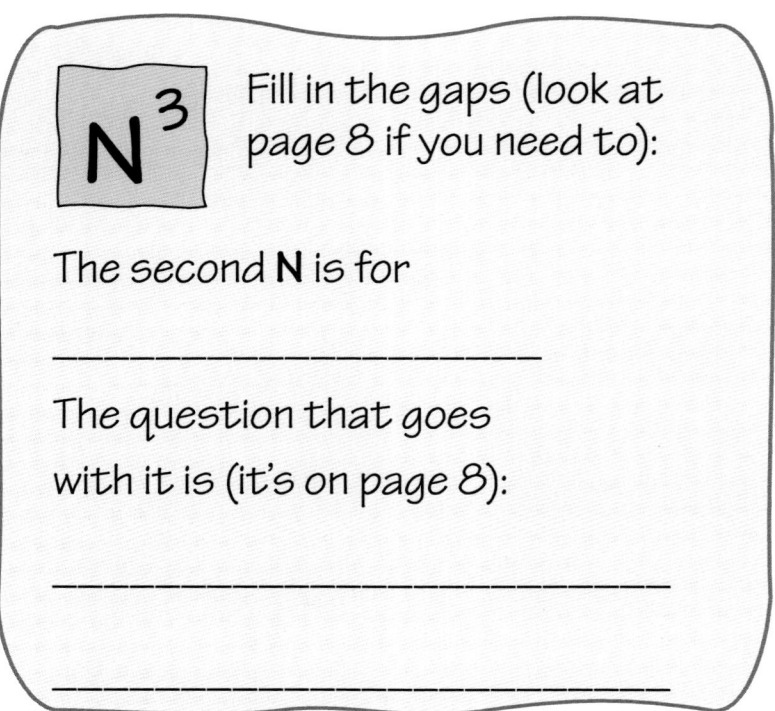

Get to know bravery

NOTICE IT
where do I feel it in my body?

Answer the questions about bravery on the left, after you've done this, draw your bravery in the box on the right.

Where do you feel it in your body? _____

Does bravery have a colour? _____

Does it have a shape? _____

How big or small is it?_____

Is it moving or still? _____

Does it have a temperature? _____

Does it have a texture, smell, and/or taste?

_____

A sound? _____

Anything else to say about bravery? _____

_____

Draw your bravery here using colours, shapes, dots, lines, and/or squiggles:

Move your body to lift your mood

Being active and moving your body helps you cope when you need to do something brave.

Write or draw ways of being active that you enjoy below:

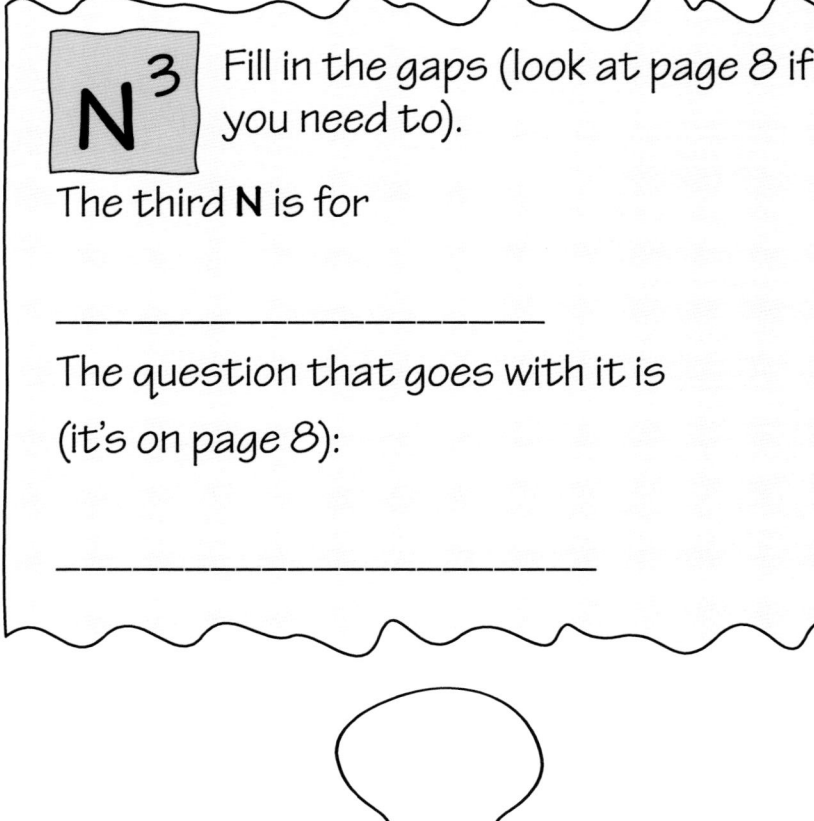

N³ Fill in the gaps (look at page 8 if you need to).

The third **N** is for

_____

The question that goes with it is (it's on page 8):

_____

Draw colours, shapes, dots, lines, and/or squiggles on the body outline above, to show how it feels when you are active.

Saying encouraging things to myself

NAIL IT
what coping skill can I use?

Speaking to yourself with kind words helps lift your mood and cope when the going gets tough. Write down some encouraging messages to say to yourself to feel brave about the trip in speech bubbles 1–5. Ask a supportive adult to write you a message to say to yourself in speech bubble 6.

Say these statements to yourself on the trip too.

TRY THIS: Come back to this page when you need to feel brave. Read the messages to yourself. Take a big, deep breath after each one.

1

2

3

4

5

6

Take 5

Breathing slowly helps you cope when big feelings arrive. Try this Take 5 technique to steady yourself:

1 Stretch your hand out like a star.
2 Get your index finger ready on the other hand (that's the one you point with).
3 Begin by placing your index finger at the bottom on the outside of your thumb.
4 Take a big breath in, move your index finger up the outside of your thumb.
5 Pause at the top of your thumb.
6 As you breathe out, trace down the inside of your thumb.
7 Pause at the bottom.
8 Repeat on the next finger and then continue with the whole hand.
9 Repeat as needed.

Practise Take 5 when you feel okay in the weeks leading up to your trip. When you get used to it, try it when your body lets you know big feelings have arrived (look at page 11 to remind yourself how your body does this).

Technique means a special way of doing something that you can practise.

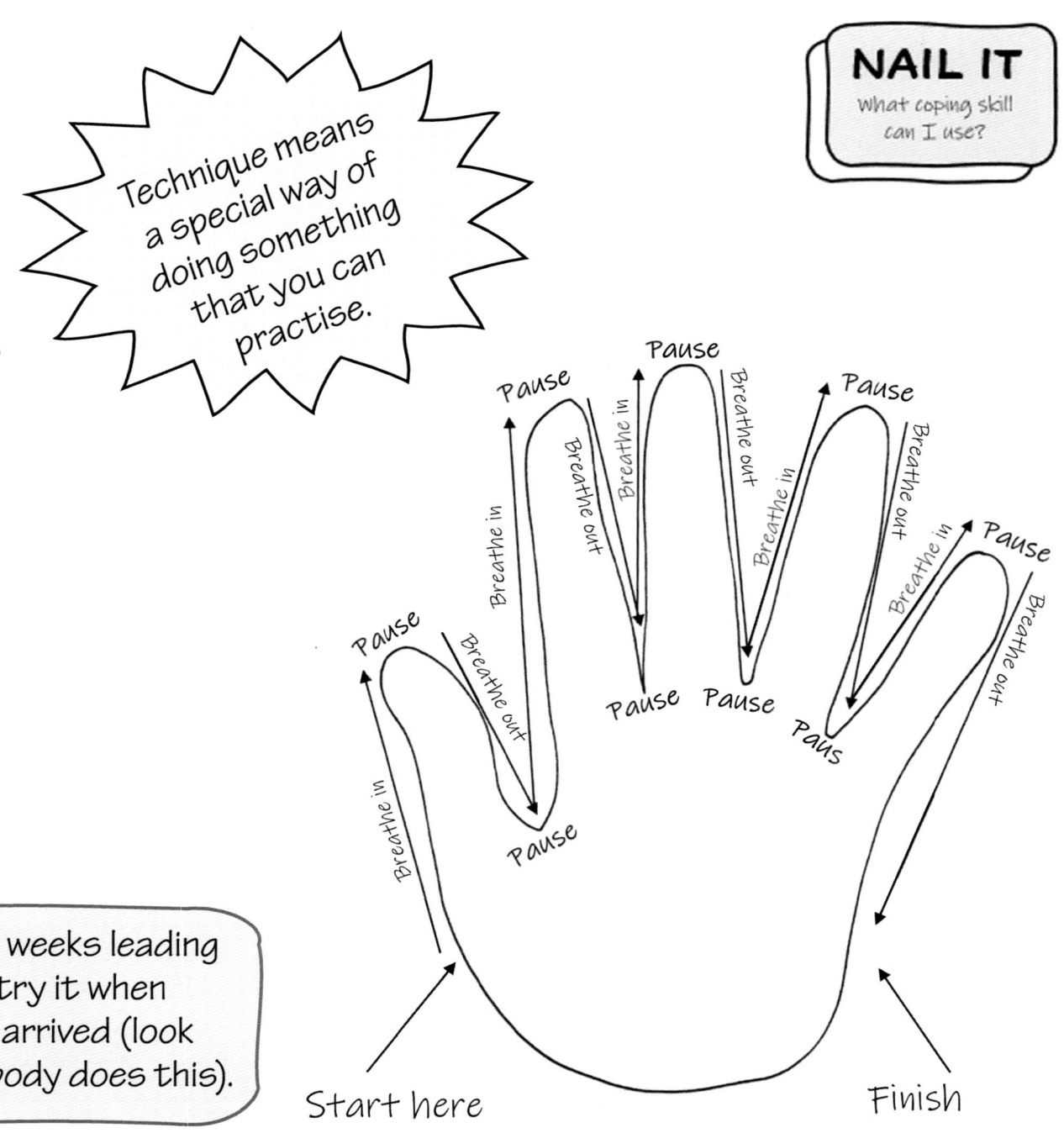

Start here

Finish

Taking my pencil for a walk

Find a pencil you'd like to draw with. Start your drawing anywhere on this page by touching your pencil to the paper. Begin to draw on the page by moving your pencil around but do not lift it off the page until you feel your drawing is done. You might like to play your favourite music as you do this. See where your hand guides you. Relax, take slow, deep breaths, and enjoy your creativity.

Do you notice any patterns or shapes? Try adding some colour to your masterpiece and any words that go with your doodle.

☺ Try this again on another piece of paper if you enjoyed it. It might be something you do whilst on the trip too. ☺

Ground yourself

NAIL IT
What coping skill can I use?

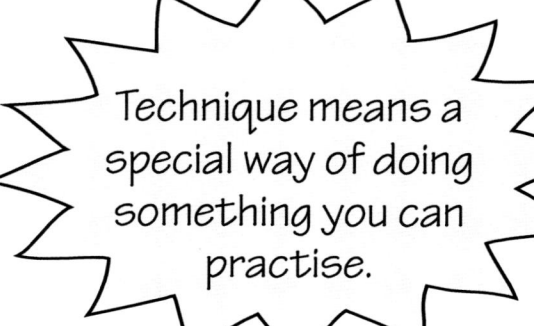
Technique means a special way of doing something you can practise.

Our minds can take us off into the future or past. Being in the present moment helps us cope and make good choices.

54321 is a technique you can use to be present by using your senses.

5

4

3

2

1

~ Take a deep breath in and out ~

Notice and name:

5 things that you can see.

4 things that you can feel.

3 things that you can hear.

2 things that you can smell or smells that you like.

1 thing that you can taste or one taste that you like

~ Take a deep breath in and out ~

Practise 54321 when you feel okay in the weeks leading up to your trip. When you get used to it, try 54321 when your body lets you know big feelings have arrived. Use this technique on the trip as needed.

Get some Vitamin N (N=Nature)

NAIL IT
what coping skill can I use?

Most likely, your residential trip will be somewhere in nature. Spending time in nature lifts your mood. Head outside with this activity book, maybe into your garden or a local park, take an adult with you or let them know where you are going. Find a place to sit.

1) Once you have found your spot, try your 54321 activity from the last page. Notice how you felt before and after doing this.
2) Wander out a little from your spot and collect what you can see on the ground. This might be twigs, leaves, fallen flowers, and/or stones. Breathe slowly as you move around. Bring the items back to your spot and arrange them in an interesting way.
3) Draw or add a photograph of your creation in the box below. Give it a name on the line at the bottom.

4) Write three words that go with your time in nature today in the star below.

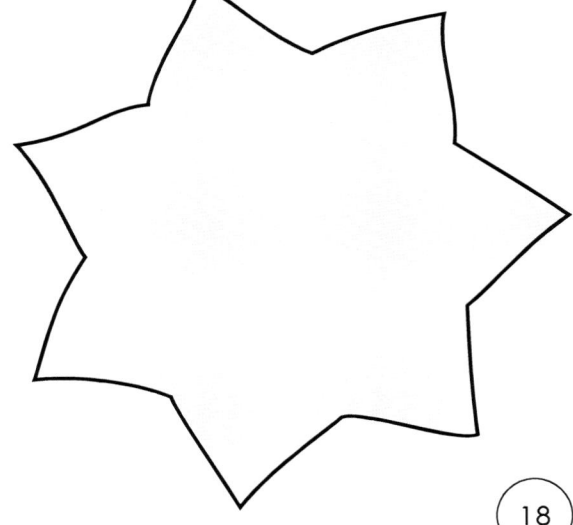

18

Thankfulness Tree

Paying attention to things you feel thankful for lifts your mood.

Write or draw ten things you are thankful for in each of the thankfulness tree leaves on the right.

TRY THIS:

1) Read one of your leaves out loud; 'I am thankful for...' (say what's on your leaf).
2) Close your eyes and imagine whatever is on that leaf.
3) Take a big breath in through your nose and breathe out through your mouth.

REPEAT FOR THE REST OF THE LEAVES.

Practice this in the weeks before and during your trip.

NAIL IT
What coping skill can I use?

My supporters

We all need help sometimes. Think of three people you can ask for help when things are tough. Write their names, one on each of the lines below the body outline that represents them. Feel free to make your people look more interesting by colouring them in.

Write down any other supporters you can talk to here:

NAIL IT

what coping skill can I use?

20

Make a Glitter Jar

When you have made your jar, you can use it to settle your mind and help you relax. The glitter in your jar is like thoughts in your mind. When you feel stressed, your mind gets all churned up. When you are calm your mind is more settled.

Gather your 'ingredients':

- One airtight PLASTIC jar with water – tight lid.
  To be safe, don't use a glass jar.
- Warm water.
- Clear glue.
- Lollypop stick.
- Glitter of various colours and sizes.

Making your jar:

1) Prepare some warm water.
2) Pour enough glitter into the jar to generously cover the bottom.
3) Add a big dollop of clear glue.
4) Add enough warm water to cover the glitter and glue and stir with the lollypop stick.
5) Put the lid on the jar and shake well.
6) Take the lid off and add water to the top, replace the lid and shake again.

Optional – Add the label at the top right of this page to the lid of your jar.

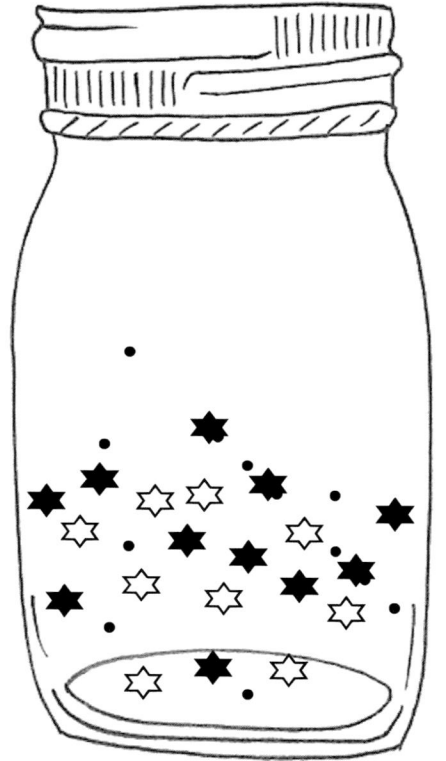

NAIL IT

what coping skill can I use?

Download the label below and stick it on your jar lid.

GLITTER JAR
(DO NOT DRINK ME)

The glitter in this jar is like thoughts in your mind. When you feel stressed, your mind gets churned up. When you are calm, your mind is more settled.

TO STEADY YOURSELF

1) Shake your jar
2) Watch the glitter settle whilst you breathe slowly

How to use your jar:

- Find a comfortable place.
- Take a deep breath.
- Shake your jar.
- Watch the glitter settle as you breathe slowly.
- Take another deep breath.

Make and practice with your jar well before your trip. You might like to take it with you when you go. Make sure you pack it carefully.

My safe place

NAIL IT
what coping skill
can I use?

Your imagination is powerful. When you think about a place where you feel safe, real or imagined, your body, heart, and mind will be positively impacted.

1) **TRY THIS:** Close your eyes. Bring an image or sense of your place into your mind. Notice what you can see, hear, touch, taste, and smell as if you were there.

2) Now, **TRY THIS:**

Practice imagining your safe place when you feel okay to begin with to get used to it. Do this in the weeks before and during your trip. Each time you visit, be curious about what is new and the same in your safe place.

Use colours, shapes, dots, lines, and/or squiggles above to represent your safe place from the activity on the left. Add words too if you wish.

22

My coping skills

Colour in the squares on this page and the next, which contain coping skills that might help you when big feelings arrive. Different people find different things helpful.

NAIL IT
what coping skill can I use?

54321.

Draw or paint how you feel using colours, shapes, and lines.

Shake your glitter jar and breathe as you watch it settle.

Play with a fidget toy, putty, or slime.

Take your pencil for a walk on your page.

Name three things you are thankful for.

Look around you and find as many things as you can that are your favourite colour.

Name three of your strengths.

Write down or draw how you are feeling.

Do some art or make something.

23

And there's more...

NAIL IT
what coping skill can I use?

TRY THIS: Place a tick in the circle of each box on this page and the last that you have tried.

Add two ideas of your own in the dotted boxes on this page.

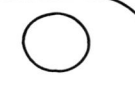 Take 5.

 Listen to music, play an instrument, or watch a movie.

 Get a drink of water and/or splash cold water on your face.

 Play with a favourite pet, friend, or toy.

Imagine your safe place.

 Talk with a trusted adult or friend.

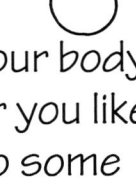 Move your body however you like e.g., do some jumping jacks, play outside, or skip.

 Say something calming to yourself like; 'It's okay, I've got this'.

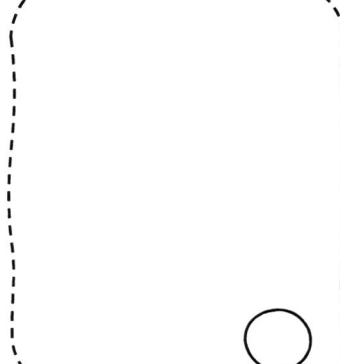

How to make a Coping Chatterbox

Get ready:

Your Chatterbox will help you choose a way of taking good care of your feelings each time you play. Before you make it, you'll need to choose eight coping strategies. These are things that help you feel steadier when the going gets tough. Use the last two pages to help you decide, or flick through this book to remind you of what helps. Write your eight coping strategies down to help you remember them before you begin making your Chatterbox.

Make it (go to the next page):

1) Write your eight coping strategies in the central triangles of your Chatterbox.
2) Colour in the colour triangles the same colour as their names (this is optional).
3) Cut out the Chatterbox by cutting the dotted line around the outside.
4) Place the Chatterbox face down with the blank side facing you.
5) Fold each corner towards the centre so the numbers and colours are facing you.
6) Turn it over and fold the corners to the middle so you see the colour names.
7) Fold it in half so that the colour names are touching and the numbers are on the outside.
8) Open it and fold it in half the other way with the numbers still facing you.
9) Insert your thumb and the first finger of each hand (pinching motion) under the number flaps.
10)   Close the Chatterbox so only the numbers show.

Play it:
- Pick a number. Open and close the Chatterbox that number of times.
- Pick a colour and spell out the colour name, opening and closing the Chatterbox for each letter.
- Choose a colour you can see and open the flap.
- Read what it says and do it.

You can play with one or two players, it's a great way to remind yourself of your coping skills.

Make and practice with your Coping Chatterbox well before your trip.
You might like to take it with you when you go.

NAIL IT
what coping skill
can I use?

My Coping Chatterbox

(instructions on the previous page).

Cut the Chatterbox out when the instructions tell you to by cutting along the outside dotted line.

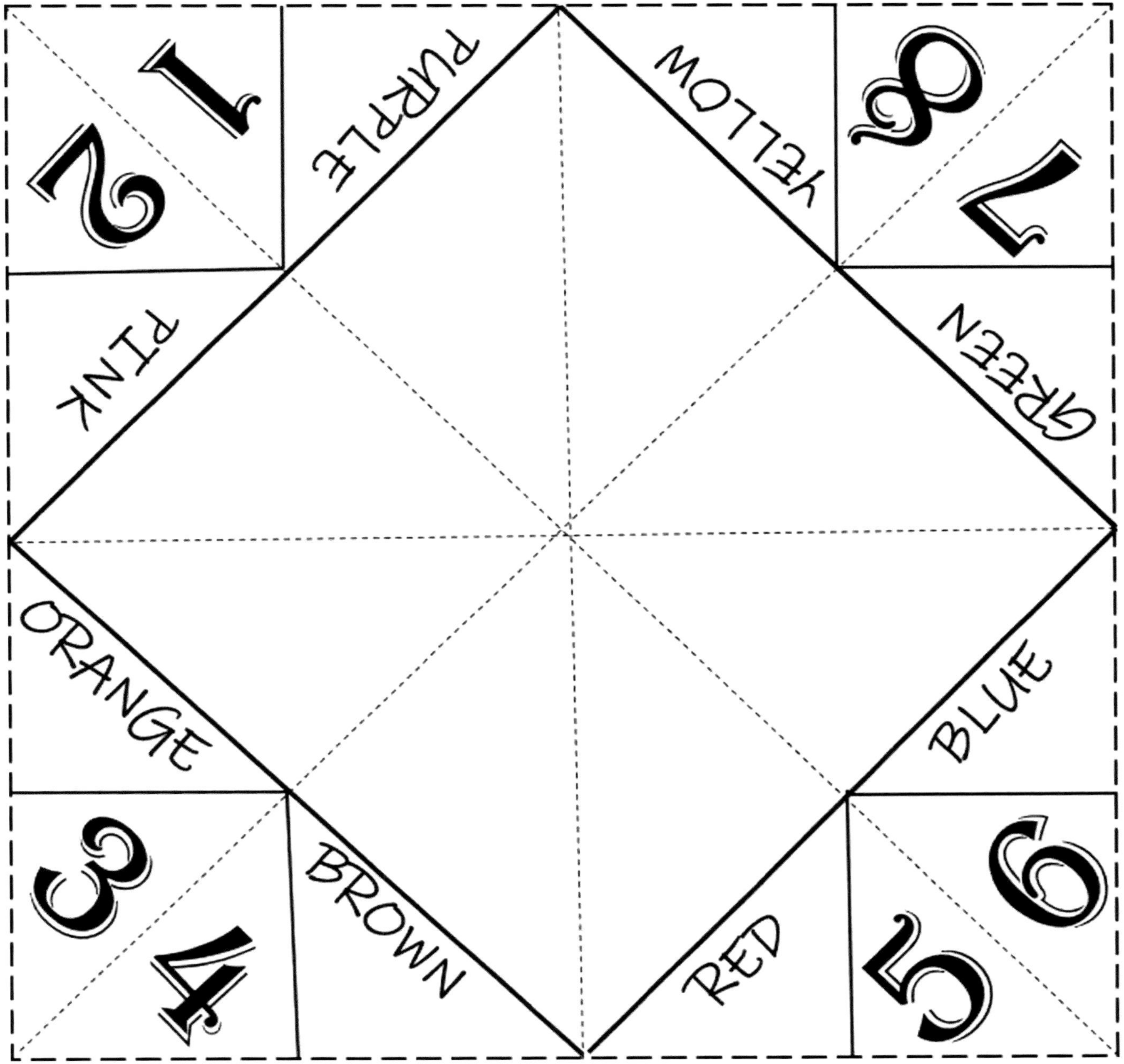
1
2
PURPLE
YELLOW
8
7
PINK
GREEN
ORANGE
BLUE
3
4
BROWN
RED
5
6

When it's made, your Chatterbox will look like this:

BROWN
ORANGE
PINK
PURPLE
BLUE
GREEN
6
7
8

Getting ready for the off

Add special things to take from home that would help you feel brave to the lid of this suitcase. Some ideas might be photos, a cuddly toy, something belonging to a family member, a fidget toy, your glitter jar, your Coping Chatterbox, or a favourite book or keepsake.

My brave bedtime plan:

Having a plan for bedtime boosts bravery. Write your plan in the sign above. Your plan may include some of the things you added to your suitcase on the left and one or two of the coping skills you've learned from this activity book.

Home Is Where the Heart Is

In the scroll below, ask a family member to write a special message to help you feel brave. Read this before and during your trip as often as you need to. You may like to download this scroll for your family member to write on, then you can take it with you on your adventure.

Talk with your family about your homecoming. Perhaps you can do something to celebrate your successful trip – maybe a favourite meal or family activity? Write your ideas below.

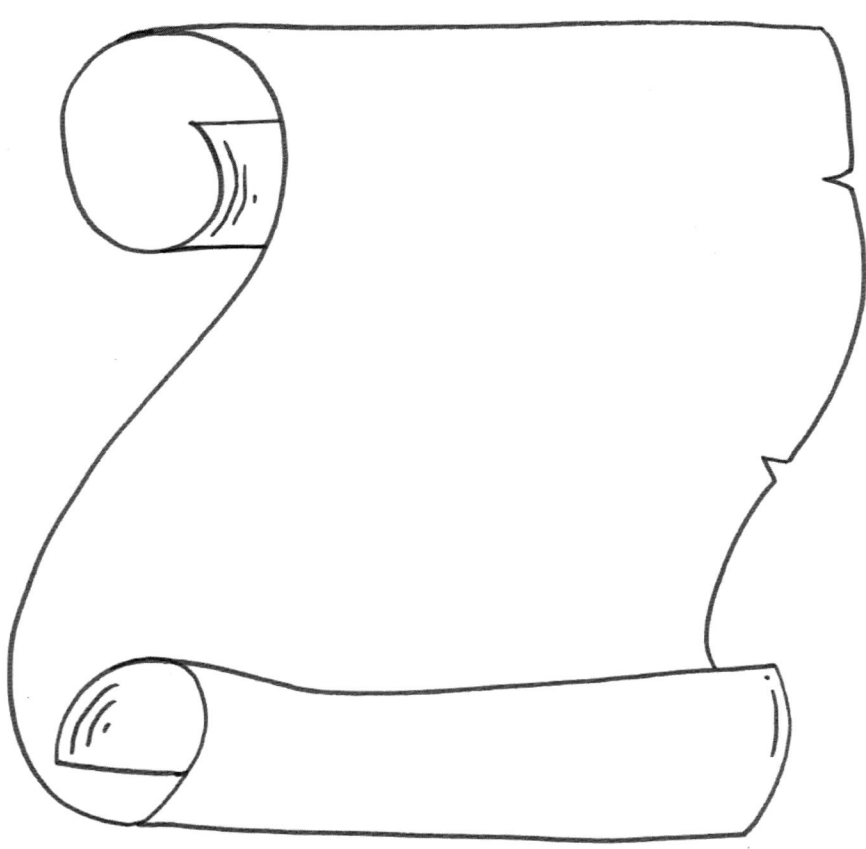

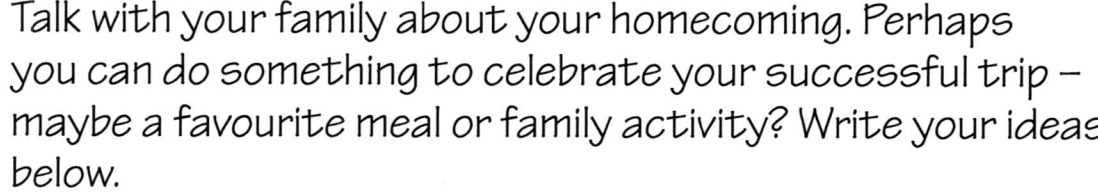

Imagine what you will say to your family about your best times on the trip. What stories might you tell?

Trip tactics

This page is to plan how you will **NAME, NOTICE,** and **NAIL** big feelings when they arrive on the trip. When it's completed, show this page to an adult who is going with you and teach them what you know. This person may be your go-to person if you need a boost of bravery whilst you are away.

NAME IT

Write a different big feeling in each of the boxes 1–3.

1)

2)

3)

NOTICE IT

Where do I feel it in my body?

NAIL IT

What coping skill will I use?

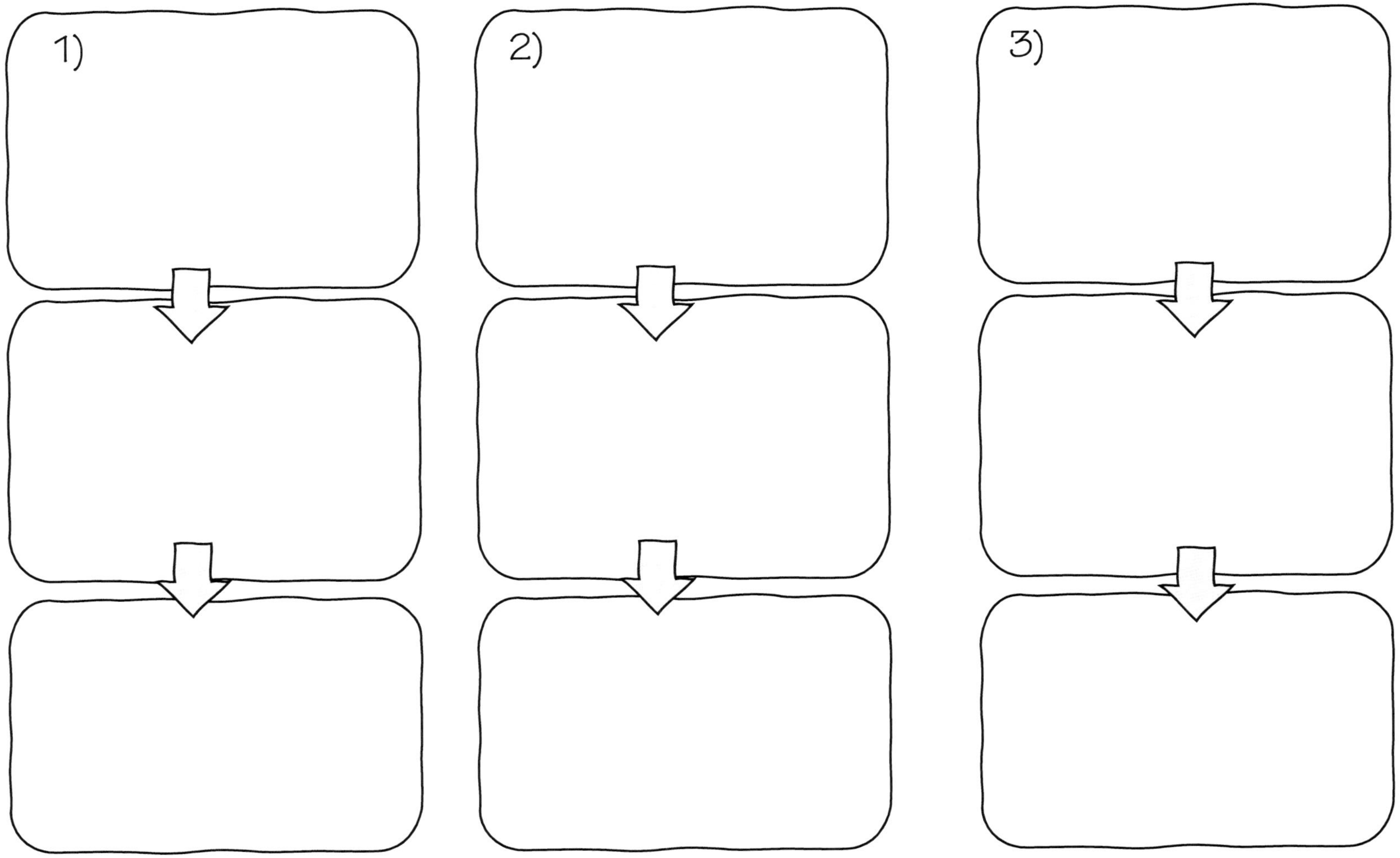

After the trip

Welcome back. Congratulations, you did it! Complete these sentences about your trip:

The bravest thing I did was _____

The hardest thing was_____

The most surprising thing was _____

The best thing I did was _____

One strength I used a lot was _____

The best thing I ate was _____

The best time with my friends was _____

The thing I am most proud of is _____

Write an encouraging message to someone who is worried about going on this trip:

Magic memories: Highlight reel

There are five spaces on the highlight reel below for you to write, draw, or add photos of five happy memories from your trip.

Technique means a special way of doing something you can practise.

TRY THIS: Magic memories technique. You may like to tune in more deeply to these times. Close your eyes, take a breath, and imagine yourself and your friend in one of your memories above. Tune into your five senses as you do this by noticing what you could see, hear, touch, smell, and taste at the time of your chosen memory. Take a deep breath and open your eyes. Repeat for your other highlight reel memories if you wish.

Winning podium

The activities in this book awakened bravery for your trip. Flick through your book, look at the pages you completed. Now, write down three things you'd like to remember about building bravery in the boxes below.

Rank them 1–3 with number 1 being the most helpful.

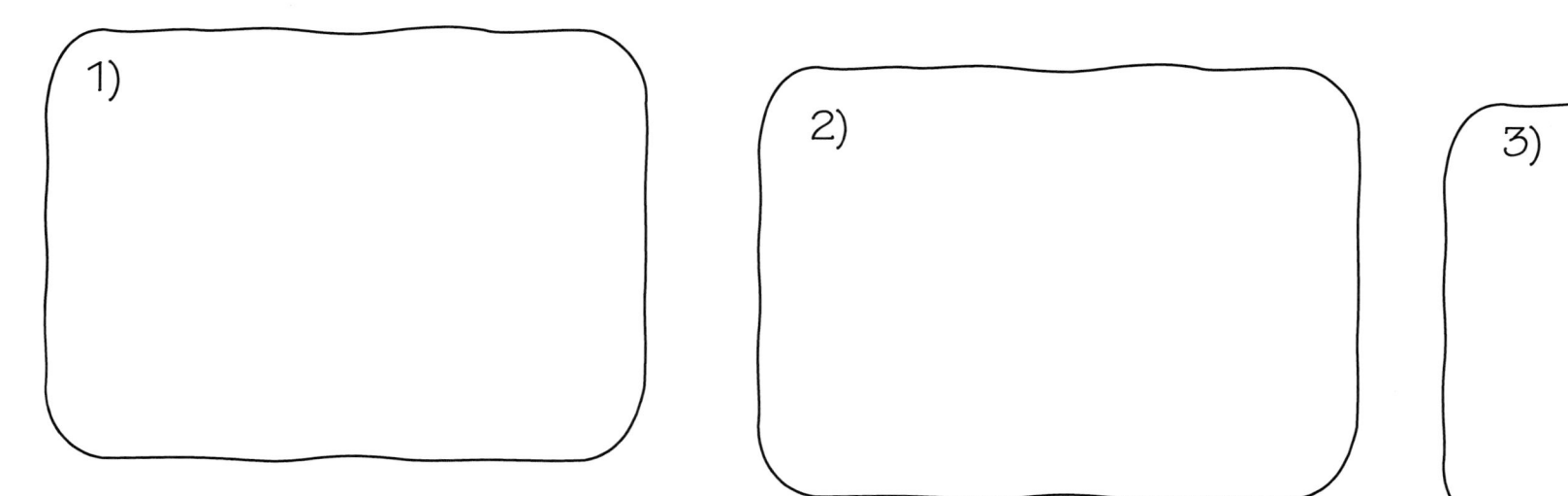

1)

2)

3)

Ask someone to write a message here to celebrate your bravery:

Awards Ceremony

Read the stickers below. Choose a page from this activity book that goes with each of them. Colour in the sticker, cut it out and glue it onto your chosen page.

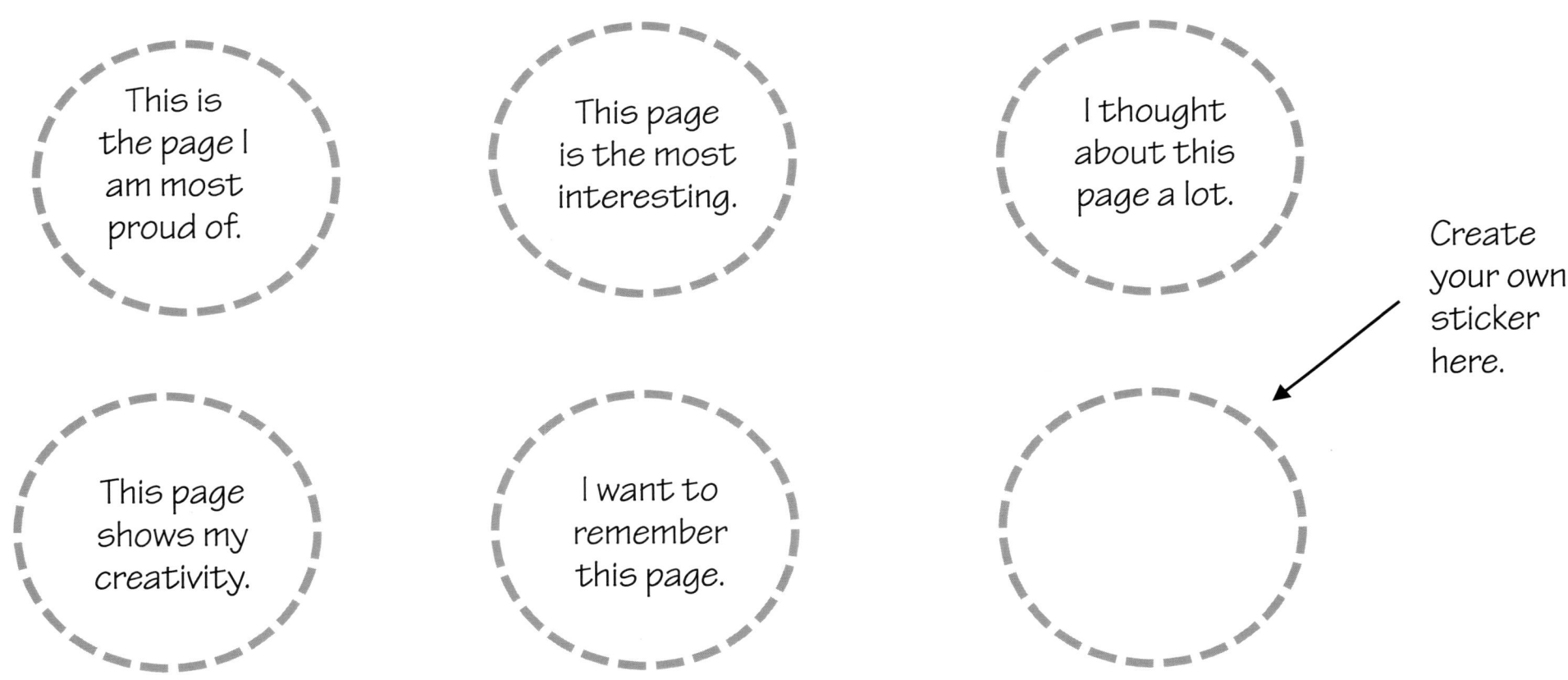

This is the page I am most proud of.

This page is the most interesting.

I thought about this page a lot.

Create your own sticker here.

This page shows my creativity.

I want to remember this page.

The back of this page is blank so that you can cut out the circles. You may prefer to download them instead.

'Brain dump' page. Add any thoughts, scribbles, or notes: